TROMBONE

BROADWAY FAVORITES

Solos and Band Arrangements
Correlated with Essential Elements Band Method

Arranged by
MICHAEL SWEENEY

Welcome to Essential Elements Broadway Favorites! There are two versions of each selection in this versatile book. The SOLO version appears in the beginning of each student book. The FULL BAND arrangements of each song follows. The supplemental CD recording or PIANO ACCOMPANIMENT BOOK may be used as an accompaniment for solo performance. Use these recordings when playing solos for friends and family.

ISBN 978-0-7935-9852-6

HAL•LEONARD®
CORPORATION
7777 W. BLUEMOUND RD. P.O. BOX 13819 MILWAUKEE, WI 53213

00860046

From Walt Disney's BEAUTY AND THE BEAST: THE BROADWAY MUSICAL

BEAUTY AND THE BEAST

TROMBONE
Solo

Lyrics by HOWARD ASHMAN
Music by ALAN MENKEN
Arranged by MICHAEL SWEENEY

00860046

From the Musical Production ANNIE

TOMORROW

TROMBONE
Solo

Lyric by MARTIN CHARNIN
Music by CHARLES STROUSE
Arranged by MICHAEL SWEENEY

From the Musical CABARET

CABARET

TROMBONE
Solo

Words by FRED EBB
Music by JOHN KANDER
Arranged by MICHAEL SWEENEY

From THE SOUND OF MUSIC

EDELWEISS

TROMBONE
Solo

Lyrics by OSCAR HAMMERSTEIN II
Music by RICHARD RODGERS
Arranged by MICHAEL SWEENEY

00860046

From EVITA

DON'T CRY FOR ME ARGENTINA

TROMBONE
Solo

Words by TIM RICE
Music by ANDREW LLOYD WEBBER
Arranged by MICHAEL SWEENEY

From MY FAIR LADY

GET ME TO THE CHURCH ON TIME

TROMBONE
Solo

Words by ALAN JAY LERNER
Music by FREDERICK LOEWE
Arranged by MICHAEL SWEENEY

00860046

From LES MISÉRABLES

I DREAMED A DREAM

Music by CLAUDE-MICHEL SCHÖNBERG
Lyrics by ALAIN BOUBLIL,
JEAN-MARC NATEL and HERBERT KRETZMER
Arranged by MICHAEL SWEENEY

TROMBONE
Solo

Gently
3
4
mf
12
20
Play lower notes if possible
f
30
mf
39
f
47
ff
mf
mp
rit.

From JOSEPH AND THE AMAZING TECHNICOLOR DREAMCOAT

GO GO GO JOSEPH

TROMBONE
Solo

Music by ANDREW LLOYD WEBBER
Lyrics by TIM RICE
Arranged by MICHAEL SWEENEY

From CATS

MEMORY

TROMBONE
Solo

Music by ANDREW LLOYD WEBBER
Text by TREVOR NUNN after T.S. ELIOT
Arranged by MICHAEL SWEENEY

From THE PHANTOM OF THE OPERA

THE PHANTOM OF THE OPERA

TROMBONE
Solo

Music by ANDREW LLOYD WEBBER
Lyrics by CHARLES HART
Additional Lyrics by RICHARD STILGOE and MIKE BATT
Arranged by MICHAEL SWEENEY

Boldly

f
11
19
Play lower notes if possible
27
mp
35
f
43
mf
f
51
mf
4

From Meredith Willson's THE MUSIC MAN

SEVENTY SIX TROMBONES

TROMBONE
Solo

By MEREDITH WILLSON
Arranged by MICHAEL SWEENEY

From Walt Disney's BEAUTY AND THE BEAST: THE BROADWAY MUSICAL

BEAUTY AND THE BEAST

TROMBONE
Band Arrangement

Lyrics by HOWARD ASHMAN
Music by ALAN MENKEN
Arranged by MICHAEL SWEENEY

From the Musical Production ANNIE

TOMORROW

TROMBONE
Band Arrangement

Lyric by MARTIN CHARNIN
Music by CHARLES STROUSE
Arranged by MICHAEL SWEENEY

00860046

From the Musical CABARET

CABARET

TROMBONE
Band Arrangement

Words by FRED EBB
Music by JOHN KANDER
Arranged by MICHAEL SWEENEY

From THE SOUND OF MUSIC

EDELWEISS

TROMBONE
Band Arrangement

Lyrics by OSCAR HAMMERSTEIN II
Music by RICHARD RODGERS
Arranged by MICHAEL SWEENEY

From EVITA

DON'T CRY FOR ME ARGENTINA

TROMBONE
Band Arrangement

Words by TIM RICE
Music by ANDREW LLOYD WEBBER
Arranged by MICHAEL SWEENEY

From MY FAIR LADY

GET ME TO THE CHURCH ON TIME

TROMBONE
Band Arrangement

Words by ALAN JAY LERNER
Music by FREDERICK LOEWE
Arranged by MICHAEL SWEENEY

From LES MISÉRABLES

I DREAMED A DREAM

TROMBONE
Band Arrangement

Music by CLAUDE-MICHEL SCHÖNBERG
Lyrics by ALAIN BOUBLIL,
JEAN-MARC NATEL and HERBERT KRETZMER
Arranged by MICHAEL SWEENEY

00860046

From JOSEPH AND THE AMAZING TECHNICOLOR DREAMCOAT

GO GO GO JOSEPH

TROMBONE
Band Arrangement

Music by ANDREW LLOYD WEBBER
Lyrics by TIM RICE
Arranged by MICHAEL SWEENEY

From CATS

MEMORY

TROMBONE
Band Arrangement

Music by ANDREW LLOYD WEBBER
Text by TREVOR NUNN after T.S. ELIOT
Arranged by MICHAEL SWEENEY

From THE PHANTOM OF THE OPERA

THE PHANTOM OF THE OPERA

TROMBONE
Band Arrangement

Music by ANDREW LLOYD WEBBER
Lyrics by CHARLES HART
Additional Lyrics by RICHARD STILGOE and MIKE BATT
Arranged by MICHAEL SWEENEY

From Meredith Willson's THE MUSIC MAN

SEVENTY SIX TROMBONES

TROMBONE
Band Arrangement

By MEREDITH WILLSON
Arranged by MICHAEL SWEENEY